50 Premium Dinner Meals for the House

By: Kelly Johnson

Table of Contents

- Filet Mignon with Garlic Herb Butter
- Lobster Tail with Lemon Garlic Butter
- Braised Short Ribs with Red Wine Reduction
- Pan-Seared Salmon with Dill Cream Sauce
- Chicken Marsala with Wild Mushrooms
- Rack of Lamb with Rosemary and Thyme
- Beef Wellington with Puff Pastry Crust
- Grilled Ribeye with Truffle Mashed Potatoes
- Stuffed Chicken Breast with Spinach & Ricotta
- Seafood Paella with Saffron Rice
- Pork Tenderloin with Apple Chutney
- Duck Breast with Orange Glaze
- Crab-Stuffed Flounder with Lemon Butter Sauce
- Gourmet Mac & Cheese with Gruyère & Lobster
- Spaghetti Carbonara with Pancetta & Parmesan
- Miso Glazed Black Cod with Bok Choy
- Cajun Shrimp & Grits with Smoked Gouda
- Osso Buco with Gremolata & Risotto Milanese
- Truffle Risotto with Parmesan & Wild Mushrooms
- Korean BBQ Short Ribs with Kimchi Slaw
- Honey Glazed Duck Confit with Sweet Potato Purée
- Saffron Butter Scallops with Asparagus
- Moroccan Lamb Tagine with Apricots & Almonds
- Smoked Brisket with Bourbon BBQ Sauce
- Eggplant Parmesan with Fresh Basil
- French Coq au Vin with Red Wine Sauce
- Coconut Curry Shrimp with Jasmine Rice
- Teriyaki Glazed Salmon with Sesame Rice
- Argentinian Chimichurri Steak with Roasted Potatoes
- Vegetable Ratatouille with Goat Cheese
- Baked Ziti with Italian Sausage & Ricotta
- Thai Green Curry Chicken with Coconut Rice
- Stuffed Peppers with Quinoa & Ground Turkey
- Balsamic Glazed Pork Chops with Roasted Pears
- Crab Cakes with Lemon Aioli & Arugula Salad

- Grilled Swordfish with Mango Salsa
- Japanese Wagyu Steak with Garlic Fried Rice
- Butter Chicken with Naan & Basmati Rice
- Braised Lamb Shanks with Garlic Mashed Potatoes
- Spanish Chorizo & Seafood Jambalaya
- Tandoori Chicken with Mint Yogurt Sauce
- Homemade Gnocchi with Pesto Cream Sauce
- Blackened Mahi-Mahi with Avocado Crema
- New Orleans Crawfish Étouffée
- Pulled Pork Sliders with Pickled Slaw
- Italian Lasagna with Béchamel & Bolognese
- Mediterranean Grilled Chicken with Hummus & Tabbouleh
- Roasted Cornish Game Hen with Herb Butter
- Gochujang Glazed Pork Belly with Sesame Rice
- Grilled Octopus with Lemon & Olive Oil

Filet Mignon with Garlic Herb Butter

Ingredients:

- 2 filet mignon steaks
- 1 tbsp olive oil
- 2 tbsp butter
- 2 cloves garlic, minced
- 1 tsp fresh thyme, chopped
- 1 tsp fresh parsley, chopped
- Salt & black pepper

Instructions:

1. Pat steaks dry and season with salt and pepper.
2. Heat olive oil in a skillet over medium-high heat. Sear steaks for 3–4 minutes per side.
3. Reduce heat to low, add butter, garlic, thyme, and parsley. Baste steaks for 1 minute.
4. Remove from heat and rest for 5 minutes before serving.

Lobster Tail with Lemon Garlic Butter

Ingredients:

- 2 lobster tails
- 2 tbsp butter, melted
- 2 cloves garlic, minced
- 1 tbsp lemon juice
- 1 tsp parsley, chopped
- Salt & black pepper

Instructions:

1. Preheat oven to 400°F (200°C). Cut lobster tails down the center and pull the meat slightly out of the shell.
2. Mix butter, garlic, and lemon juice, then brush onto the lobster meat.
3. Place lobster tails on a baking sheet and bake for 10–12 minutes, basting once with butter mixture.
4. Garnish with parsley and serve immediately.

Braised Short Ribs with Red Wine Reduction

Ingredients:

- 2 lbs beef short ribs
- 1 tbsp olive oil
- 1 onion, chopped
- 2 carrots, chopped
- 2 cloves garlic, minced
- 1 cup red wine
- 2 cups beef broth
- 1 tsp thyme
- Salt & black pepper

Instructions:

1. Preheat oven to 325°F (165°C).
2. Season short ribs with salt and pepper. Heat olive oil in a Dutch oven and sear ribs on all sides. Remove and set aside.
3. Sauté onions, carrots, and garlic until softened.
4. Pour in red wine, scraping up browned bits. Add broth, thyme, and short ribs.
5. Cover and braise in the oven for 3 hours until tender.

Pan-Seared Salmon with Dill Cream Sauce

Ingredients:

- 2 salmon fillets
- 1 tbsp olive oil
- Salt & black pepper
- **For Sauce:**
    - 1/2 cup heavy cream
    - 1 tbsp lemon juice
    - 1 tbsp fresh dill, chopped

Instructions:

1. Heat olive oil in a pan over medium-high heat. Season salmon with salt and black pepper.
2. Sear for 3–4 minutes per side until golden brown. Remove and keep warm.
3. Simmer cream, lemon juice, and dill in the same pan for 2 minutes.
4. Drizzle sauce over salmon and serve.

Chicken Marsala with Wild Mushrooms

Ingredients:

- 2 chicken breasts
- 1/2 cup flour
- 1 cup wild mushrooms, sliced
- 1/2 cup Marsala wine
- 1/2 cup chicken broth
- 2 tbsp butter
- Salt & black pepper

Instructions:

1. Dredge chicken in flour and season with salt and pepper.
2. Sear in butter for 4 minutes per side until golden brown. Remove and set aside.
3. Sauté mushrooms, then deglaze with Marsala wine.
4. Add chicken broth and return chicken to the pan. Simmer for 5 minutes.

Rack of Lamb with Rosemary and Thyme

Ingredients:

- 1 rack of lamb
- 2 cloves garlic, minced
- 1 tbsp fresh rosemary, chopped
- 1 tbsp fresh thyme, chopped
- 2 tbsp olive oil
- Salt & black pepper

Instructions:

1. Preheat oven to 400°F (200°C).
2. Rub lamb with garlic, rosemary, thyme, olive oil, salt, and pepper.
3. Sear in a hot pan for 3 minutes per side, then roast for 20–25 minutes for medium-rare.
4. Rest for 5 minutes before slicing.

Beef Wellington with Puff Pastry Crust

Ingredients:

- 1 beef tenderloin
- 1/2 cup mushrooms, finely chopped
- 1 tbsp Dijon mustard
- 4 slices prosciutto
- 1 sheet puff pastry
- 1 egg yolk (for egg wash)

Instructions:

1. Sear beef in a hot pan for 2 minutes per side. Let cool and brush with mustard.
2. Spread mushrooms over prosciutto, then wrap around beef.
3. Wrap in puff pastry, brush with egg wash, and bake at 400°F (200°C) for 25 minutes.

Grilled Ribeye with Truffle Mashed Potatoes

Ingredients:

- 2 ribeye steaks
- 1 tbsp olive oil
- **For Potatoes:**
    - 2 cups mashed potatoes
    - 1 tsp truffle oil
    - 2 tbsp butter

Instructions:

1. Season steaks with salt and pepper. Grill for 4 minutes per side.
2. Mix mashed potatoes with truffle oil and butter. Serve alongside steaks.

Stuffed Chicken Breast with Spinach & Ricotta

Ingredients:

- 2 chicken breasts
- 1/2 cup ricotta cheese
- 1/2 cup spinach, chopped
- 1/2 tsp garlic powder
- Salt & black pepper

Instructions:

1. Slice chicken to create a pocket.
2. Mix ricotta, spinach, garlic powder, salt, and pepper. Stuff into chicken and secure with toothpicks.
3. Sear in a pan for 3 minutes per side, then bake at 375°F (190°C) for 15 minutes.

Seafood Paella with Saffron Rice

Ingredients:

- 1 cup Arborio or Bomba rice
- 2 cups seafood broth
- 1/2 tsp saffron threads
- 1/2 lb shrimp, peeled and deveined
- 1/2 lb mussels, cleaned
- 1/2 lb squid, sliced
- 1/2 onion, chopped
- 2 cloves garlic, minced
- 1/2 cup bell peppers, diced
- 1/2 cup tomatoes, diced
- 1/2 tsp smoked paprika
- 1 tbsp olive oil
- 1/4 cup peas

Instructions:

1. Heat olive oil in a large pan. Sauté onion, garlic, and bell peppers until soft.
2. Stir in rice, smoked paprika, and saffron, cooking for 1 minute.
3. Add diced tomatoes and seafood broth, simmering for 10 minutes.
4. Nestle in shrimp, mussels, and squid, cooking until mussels open and shrimp are opaque.
5. Sprinkle peas over the top and serve.

Pork Tenderloin with Apple Chutney

Ingredients:

- 1 lb pork tenderloin
- 1 tbsp olive oil
- 1/2 tsp salt
- 1/2 tsp black pepper
- **For Chutney:**
    - 1 apple, peeled and diced
    - 1/4 cup brown sugar
    - 1/4 cup apple cider vinegar
    - 1/4 tsp cinnamon

Instructions:

1. Preheat oven to 375°F (190°C).
2. Season pork with salt and pepper, then sear in olive oil until browned.
3. Transfer to the oven and roast for 20 minutes.
4. Meanwhile, simmer chutney ingredients until apples are soft.
5. Slice pork and serve with chutney.

Duck Breast with Orange Glaze

Ingredients:

- 2 duck breasts
- 1/2 tsp salt
- 1/2 tsp black pepper
- **For Glaze:**
    - 1/2 cup orange juice
    - 1 tbsp honey
    - 1 tbsp balsamic vinegar

Instructions:

1. Score the skin of the duck breasts, season with salt and pepper.
2. Place skin-side down in a cold pan, then heat to medium and sear for 6 minutes. Flip and cook for 3 more minutes.
3. Remove duck and rest. In the same pan, simmer orange juice, honey, and balsamic vinegar until thickened.
4. Slice duck and drizzle with glaze.

Crab-Stuffed Flounder with Lemon Butter Sauce

Ingredients:

- 2 flounder fillets
- 1/2 cup lump crab meat
- 2 tbsp breadcrumbs
- 1 tbsp mayonnaise
- 1 tsp Dijon mustard
- 1 tbsp parsley, chopped
- **For Lemon Butter Sauce:**
    - 2 tbsp butter
    - 1 tbsp lemon juice
    - 1 clove garlic, minced

Instructions:

1. Preheat oven to 375°F (190°C).
2. Mix crab, breadcrumbs, mayonnaise, mustard, and parsley.
3. Spoon filling onto flounder fillets, roll up, and place in a baking dish.
4. Melt butter, mix with lemon juice and garlic, and drizzle over fillets.
5. Bake for 15 minutes until cooked through.

Gourmet Mac & Cheese with Gruyère & Lobster

Ingredients:

- 8 oz elbow macaroni
- 1 cup cooked lobster meat, chopped
- 2 tbsp butter
- 2 tbsp flour
- 2 cups whole milk
- 1 cup Gruyère cheese, shredded
- 1/2 cup sharp cheddar cheese, shredded
- 1/2 tsp Dijon mustard
- 1/2 cup panko breadcrumbs

Instructions:

1. Cook pasta, drain, and set aside.
2. Melt butter in a saucepan, whisk in flour, then gradually add milk.
3. Stir in Gruyère, cheddar, and mustard until smooth.
4. Combine with pasta and lobster, then transfer to a baking dish.
5. Sprinkle with panko and bake at 375°F (190°C) for 15 minutes.

Spaghetti Carbonara with Pancetta & Parmesan

Ingredients:

- 12 oz spaghetti
- 4 oz pancetta, diced
- 2 eggs
- 1/2 cup Parmesan cheese, grated
- 1 clove garlic, minced
- Black pepper to taste

Instructions:

1. Cook spaghetti and reserve 1/2 cup pasta water.
2. Sauté pancetta and garlic until crispy.
3. Whisk eggs, Parmesan, and black pepper.
4. Toss hot pasta with pancetta, then quickly mix in egg mixture, adding pasta water as needed.

Miso Glazed Black Cod with Bok Choy

Ingredients:

- 2 black cod fillets
- 2 tbsp white miso paste
- 1 tbsp soy sauce
- 1 tbsp honey
- 1 tsp sesame oil
- 2 heads baby bok choy, halved
- 1 tbsp vegetable oil

Instructions:

1. Mix miso paste, soy sauce, honey, and sesame oil.
2. Marinate cod in the mixture for at least 1 hour.
3. Preheat oven to 400°F (200°C) and bake cod for 12–15 minutes.
4. Sauté bok choy in vegetable oil for 3 minutes and serve alongside cod.

Cajun Shrimp & Grits with Smoked Gouda

Ingredients:

- 1/2 lb shrimp, peeled
- 1 tbsp Cajun seasoning
- 1 tbsp butter
- **For Grits:**
    - 1 cup grits
    - 2 cups chicken broth
    - 1/2 cup smoked Gouda cheese, shredded

Instructions:

1. Cook grits in chicken broth, then stir in Gouda.
2. Toss shrimp with Cajun seasoning and sauté in butter for 3 minutes per side.
3. Serve shrimp over creamy grits.

Osso Buco with Gremolata & Risotto Milanese

Ingredients:

- **For Osso Buco:**
    - 2 veal shanks
    - 1/2 cup white wine
    - 2 cups beef broth
    - 1 onion, chopped
    - 1 carrot, chopped
    - 2 cloves garlic, minced
    - 1 tsp thyme
- **For Gremolata:**
    - 1 tbsp parsley, chopped
    - 1 tsp lemon zest
    - 1 clove garlic, minced
- **For Risotto Milanese:**
    - 1 cup Arborio rice
    - 3 cups chicken broth
    - 1/2 tsp saffron
    - 1/2 cup Parmesan cheese, grated

Instructions:

1. Sear veal shanks, then remove.
2. Sauté onion, carrot, and garlic. Add wine, broth, and thyme. Return veal and braise at 325°F (165°C) for 2.5 hours.
3. Mix gremolata ingredients and sprinkle over osso buco before serving.
4. Cook risotto by gradually adding broth and saffron while stirring. Stir in Parmesan before serving with osso buco.

Truffle Risotto with Parmesan & Wild Mushrooms

Ingredients:

- 1 cup Arborio rice
- 3 cups chicken broth
- 1/2 cup wild mushrooms, sliced
- 1/2 cup Parmesan cheese, grated
- 1 tsp truffle oil
- 1 tbsp butter

Instructions:

1. Sauté mushrooms in butter, then add Arborio rice.
2. Gradually add broth, stirring constantly until absorbed.
3. Stir in Parmesan and drizzle with truffle oil before serving.

Korean BBQ Short Ribs with Kimchi Slaw

Ingredients:

- 1 lb beef short ribs
- 1/4 cup soy sauce
- 2 tbsp brown sugar
- 1 tbsp sesame oil
- **For Kimchi Slaw:**
    - 1/2 cup kimchi, chopped
    - 1/2 cup shredded cabbage
    - 1 tbsp rice vinegar

Instructions:

1. Marinate short ribs in soy sauce, brown sugar, and sesame oil for 2 hours.
2. Grill short ribs for 4 minutes per side.
3. Mix slaw ingredients and serve with ribs.

Honey Glazed Duck Confit with Sweet Potato Purée

Ingredients:

- 2 duck legs
- 1 tsp salt
- **For Glaze:**
    - 2 tbsp honey
    - 1 tbsp balsamic vinegar
- **For Sweet Potato Purée:**
    - 2 sweet potatoes, peeled and mashed
    - 1/4 cup heavy cream
    - 1 tbsp butter

Instructions:

1. Rub duck with salt and slow cook at 250°F (120°C) for 3 hours.
2. Brush with honey glaze and broil for 5 minutes.
3. Mix mashed sweet potatoes with cream and butter. Serve with duck.

Saffron Butter Scallops with Asparagus

Ingredients:

- 6 large sea scallops
- 2 tbsp butter
- 1/4 tsp saffron
- 1 bunch asparagus, trimmed

Instructions:

1. Sauté scallops in butter for 2 minutes per side.
2. Steam asparagus and serve alongside scallops.
3. Drizzle with saffron-infused butter.

Moroccan Lamb Tagine with Apricots & Almonds

Ingredients:

- 1 lb lamb shoulder, cubed
- 1 onion, chopped
- 2 cloves garlic, minced
- 1 tsp cinnamon
- 1/2 tsp cumin
- 1/2 tsp paprika
- 1/2 cup dried apricots, chopped
- 1/4 cup almonds, toasted
- 2 cups beef broth

Instructions:

1. Sear lamb in a Dutch oven, then remove.
2. Sauté onion and garlic, then add spices.
3. Return lamb, add apricots and broth, and simmer for 1.5 hours.
4. Garnish with almonds before serving.

Smoked Brisket with Bourbon BBQ Sauce

Ingredients:

- 3 lbs beef brisket
- 2 tbsp salt
- 1 tbsp black pepper
- 1 tbsp smoked paprika
- 1 cup wood chips (for smoking)
- **For BBQ Sauce:**
    - 1/2 cup bourbon
    - 1/2 cup ketchup
    - 2 tbsp brown sugar

Instructions:

1. Rub brisket with salt, pepper, and paprika.
2. Smoke at 225°F (110°C) for 6 hours.
3. Simmer BBQ sauce ingredients until thickened.
4. Slice brisket and serve with sauce.

Eggplant Parmesan with Fresh Basil

Ingredients:

- 2 eggplants, sliced
- 1 cup breadcrumbs
- 1/2 cup Parmesan cheese, grated
- 1 cup marinara sauce
- 1 cup mozzarella, shredded
- 1/4 cup fresh basil, chopped

Instructions:

1. Dip eggplant slices in breadcrumbs and bake at 375°F (190°C) for 15 minutes.
2. Layer eggplant, marinara, and cheese in a baking dish.
3. Bake for 20 minutes until bubbly, then garnish with basil.

French Coq au Vin with Red Wine Sauce

Ingredients:

- 4 bone-in chicken thighs
- 1/2 cup red wine
- 1 cup chicken broth
- 1/2 onion, chopped
- 2 cloves garlic, minced
- 1/2 cup mushrooms, sliced
- 1/4 cup pancetta, diced
- 1 tbsp butter

Instructions:

1. Sear chicken in butter, then remove.
2. Sauté pancetta, onion, garlic, and mushrooms.
3. Add wine, broth, and return chicken. Simmer for 45 minutes.

Coconut Curry Shrimp with Jasmine Rice

Ingredients:

- 1/2 lb shrimp, peeled
- 1 cup coconut milk
- 1 tbsp red curry paste
- 1 tsp ginger, minced
- 1 clove garlic, minced
- 1/2 cup bell peppers, sliced
- 1 cup jasmine rice

Instructions:

1. Cook rice and set aside.
2. Sauté garlic, ginger, and bell peppers.
3. Add curry paste, coconut milk, and shrimp. Simmer for 5 minutes.
4. Serve over jasmine rice.

Teriyaki Glazed Salmon with Sesame Rice

Ingredients:

- 2 salmon fillets
- 1/4 cup soy sauce
- 2 tbsp honey
- 1 tsp sesame oil
- 1 cup cooked rice

Instructions:

1. Mix soy sauce, honey, and sesame oil. Marinate salmon for 30 minutes.
2. Sear salmon for 3 minutes per side, then glaze with marinade.
3. Serve over rice, garnished with sesame seeds.

Argentinian Chimichurri Steak with Roasted Potatoes

Ingredients:

- 1 lb steak (ribeye or flank)
- 1 tsp salt
- 1/2 tsp black pepper
- **For Chimichurri:**
    - 1/2 cup parsley, chopped
    - 2 cloves garlic, minced
    - 1/4 cup olive oil
    - 1 tbsp red wine vinegar
- **For Potatoes:**
    - 2 cups potatoes, cubed
    - 1 tbsp olive oil

Instructions:

1. Season steak with salt and pepper. Grill for 4 minutes per side.
2. Roast potatoes at 400°F (200°C) for 25 minutes.
3. Mix chimichurri ingredients and serve over steak.

Vegetable Ratatouille with Goat Cheese

Ingredients:

- 1 zucchini, sliced
- 1 eggplant, sliced
- 1 bell pepper, chopped
- 1 tomato, sliced
- 1/2 onion, sliced
- 2 cloves garlic, minced
- 1/4 cup goat cheese, crumbled

Instructions:

1. Sauté onion and garlic.
2. Layer vegetables in a baking dish and bake at 375°F (190°C) for 25 minutes.
3. Sprinkle with goat cheese before serving.

Baked Ziti with Italian Sausage & Ricotta

Ingredients:

- 12 oz ziti pasta
- 1/2 lb Italian sausage
- 1 cup marinara sauce
- 1/2 cup ricotta cheese
- 1 cup mozzarella cheese, shredded
- 1/4 cup Parmesan cheese

Instructions:

1. Cook pasta, then mix with marinara and sausage.
2. Layer in a baking dish with ricotta and mozzarella.
3. Bake at 375°F (190°C) for 20 minutes, then sprinkle with Parmesan.

Thai Green Curry Chicken with Coconut Rice

Ingredients:

- 2 chicken breasts, sliced
- 1 tbsp green curry paste
- 1 cup coconut milk
- 1/2 cup bell peppers, sliced
- 1/2 tsp fish sauce
- 1 cup jasmine rice

Instructions:

1. Cook jasmine rice in coconut milk and water.
2. Sauté chicken and bell peppers, then add curry paste and coconut milk.
3. Simmer for 10 minutes and serve over rice.

Stuffed Peppers with Quinoa & Ground Turkey

Ingredients:

- 4 bell peppers, halved and deseeded
- 1/2 lb ground turkey
- 1 cup cooked quinoa
- 1/2 onion, chopped
- 1 clove garlic, minced
- 1/2 cup tomato sauce
- 1/2 tsp cumin
- 1/2 cup shredded mozzarella cheese

Instructions:

1. Preheat oven to 375°F (190°C).
2. Sauté onion and garlic, then add ground turkey and cook until browned.
3. Stir in quinoa, tomato sauce, and cumin.
4. Stuff peppers with the mixture, top with cheese, and bake for 25 minutes.

Balsamic Glazed Pork Chops with Roasted Pears

Ingredients:

- 2 bone-in pork chops
- 1/2 tsp salt
- 1/4 tsp black pepper
- 1/4 cup balsamic vinegar
- 1 tbsp honey
- 1 pear, sliced

Instructions:

1. Season pork chops with salt and pepper.
2. Sear in a pan for 3–4 minutes per side, then remove.
3. Add balsamic vinegar and honey to the pan, simmering until thick.
4. Roast pear slices in the glaze, return chops, and cook for 2 minutes.

Crab Cakes with Lemon Aioli & Arugula Salad

Ingredients:

- **For Crab Cakes:**
    - 1/2 lb lump crab meat
    - 1/4 cup breadcrumbs
    - 1 egg
    - 1 tbsp mayonnaise
    - 1 tsp Dijon mustard
- **For Lemon Aioli:**
    - 1/2 cup mayonnaise
    - 1 tbsp lemon juice
    - 1 clove garlic, minced
- **For Salad:**
    - 2 cups arugula
    - 1 tbsp olive oil
    - 1 tsp lemon juice

Instructions:

1. Mix crab cake ingredients, shape into patties, and pan-fry until golden brown.
2. Mix aioli ingredients and serve with crab cakes.
3. Toss arugula with olive oil and lemon juice.

Grilled Swordfish with Mango Salsa

Ingredients:

- 2 swordfish steaks
- 1 tbsp olive oil
- **For Mango Salsa:**
    - 1/2 cup mango, diced
    - 1/4 cup red onion, chopped
    - 1 tbsp lime juice
    - 1 tbsp cilantro, chopped

Instructions:

1. Brush swordfish with olive oil and grill for 4 minutes per side.
2. Mix mango salsa ingredients and serve over swordfish.

Japanese Wagyu Steak with Garlic Fried Rice

Ingredients:

- 2 Wagyu steaks
- 1 tsp salt
- **For Garlic Fried Rice:**
    - 1 cup cooked rice
    - 2 cloves garlic, minced
    - 1 tbsp soy sauce

Instructions:

1. Sear Wagyu steak for 2 minutes per side, then rest.
2. Sauté garlic, then stir in rice and soy sauce.
3. Slice steak and serve over rice.

Butter Chicken with Naan & Basmati Rice

Ingredients:

- 2 chicken breasts, cubed
- 1 tbsp butter
- 1/2 onion, chopped
- 2 cloves garlic, minced
- 1 tsp garam masala
- 1/2 tsp turmeric
- 1 cup tomato sauce
- 1/2 cup heavy cream

Instructions:

1. Sauté onion, garlic, and spices in butter.
2. Add chicken and cook for 5 minutes.
3. Stir in tomato sauce and simmer for 10 minutes.
4. Add cream and cook for 2 more minutes.
5. Serve with naan and basmati rice.

Braised Lamb Shanks with Garlic Mashed Potatoes

Ingredients:

- 2 lamb shanks
- 1 onion, chopped
- 2 cloves garlic, minced
- 1 cup red wine
- 2 cups beef broth
- 1 tsp rosemary

Instructions:

1. Sear lamb shanks, then remove.
2. Sauté onion and garlic, then deglaze with red wine.
3. Add broth and rosemary, then braise at 325°F (165°C) for 2.5 hours.

Spanish Chorizo & Seafood Jambalaya

Ingredients:

- 1/2 lb chorizo, sliced
- 1/2 lb shrimp
- 1/2 lb mussels
- 1 cup rice
- 2 cups chicken broth
- 1/2 cup bell peppers, chopped
- 1/2 tsp paprika

Instructions:

1. Sauté chorizo and bell peppers.
2. Stir in rice and broth, simmering for 15 minutes.
3. Add shrimp and mussels, cooking until mussels open.

Tandoori Chicken with Mint Yogurt Sauce

Ingredients:

- 2 chicken breasts
- 1 tbsp tandoori spice blend
- 1/2 cup yogurt
- **For Mint Sauce:**
    - 1/2 cup yogurt
    - 1 tbsp fresh mint, chopped
    - 1 tsp lemon juice

Instructions:

1. Marinate chicken in tandoori spice and yogurt for 1 hour.
2. Grill or bake at 375°F (190°C) for 25 minutes.
3. Mix mint sauce ingredients and serve with chicken.

Homemade Gnocchi with Pesto Cream Sauce

Ingredients:

- **For Gnocchi:**
    - 2 large potatoes, boiled and mashed
    - 1 cup flour
    - 1 egg
- **For Sauce:**
    - 1/2 cup heavy cream
    - 2 tbsp pesto

Instructions:

1. Mix mashed potatoes, flour, and egg into a dough. Roll and cut into gnocchi.
2. Boil until they float, then drain.
3. Heat cream and stir in pesto. Toss gnocchi in sauce.

Blackened Mahi-Mahi with Avocado Crema

Ingredients:

- 2 mahi-mahi fillets
- 1 tsp blackening seasoning
- **For Avocado Crema:**
    - 1 avocado
    - 1/4 cup sour cream
    - 1 tbsp lime juice

Instructions:

1. Season mahi-mahi and sear for 3 minutes per side.
2. Blend crema ingredients and serve over fish.

New Orleans Crawfish Étouffée

Ingredients:

- 1/2 lb crawfish tails
- 4 tbsp butter
- 1/4 cup flour
- 1/2 onion, chopped
- 1/2 bell pepper, chopped
- 2 cloves garlic, minced
- 1 cup seafood broth
- 1/2 tsp Cajun seasoning
- 1/2 tsp paprika
- 1/2 tsp hot sauce
- 1 tbsp green onions, chopped
- 1 cup cooked rice

Instructions:

1. Melt butter in a pan and whisk in flour to make a roux, stirring until golden brown.
2. Add onion, bell pepper, and garlic, cooking until softened.
3. Pour in seafood broth, then stir in Cajun seasoning, paprika, and hot sauce.
4. Add crawfish tails and simmer for 5 minutes.
5. Serve over rice and garnish with green onions.

Pulled Pork Sliders with Pickled Slaw

Ingredients:

- 1 lb pork shoulder
- 1 tsp salt
- 1/2 tsp black pepper
- 1/2 tsp smoked paprika
- 1/2 cup BBQ sauce
- **For Pickled Slaw:**
    - 1 cup shredded cabbage
    - 1/4 cup apple cider vinegar
    - 1 tbsp sugar
    - 1/2 tsp salt
- 6 slider buns

Instructions:

1. Season pork with salt, pepper, and smoked paprika. Slow cook at 275°F (135°C) for 4 hours, then shred.
2. Toss shredded pork with BBQ sauce.
3. Mix slaw ingredients and let marinate for 30 minutes.
4. Assemble sliders with pulled pork and slaw on buns.

Italian Lasagna with Béchamel & Bolognese

Ingredients:

- **For Bolognese:**
    - 1/2 lb ground beef
    - 1/2 lb Italian sausage
    - 1/2 onion, chopped
    - 2 cloves garlic, minced
    - 1 can (14 oz) crushed tomatoes
    - 1 tsp oregano
- **For Béchamel Sauce:**
    - 2 tbsp butter
    - 2 tbsp flour
    - 2 cups milk
    - 1/2 cup Parmesan cheese
- 12 lasagna noodles
- 1 cup mozzarella cheese, shredded

Instructions:

1. Sauté onion, garlic, beef, and sausage. Add tomatoes and oregano, simmer for 30 minutes.
2. Melt butter, whisk in flour, and slowly add milk to make béchamel. Stir in Parmesan.
3. Layer noodles, Bolognese, and béchamel in a baking dish, repeating layers.
4. Top with mozzarella and bake at 375°F (190°C) for 35 minutes.

Mediterranean Grilled Chicken with Hummus & Tabbouleh

Ingredients:

- **For Chicken:**
    - 2 chicken breasts
    - 2 tbsp olive oil
    - 1 tsp lemon juice
    - 1 tsp oregano
- **For Hummus:**
    - 1 can (14 oz) chickpeas
    - 2 tbsp tahini
    - 1 tbsp lemon juice
    - 1 clove garlic, minced
- **For Tabbouleh:**
    - 1 cup cooked bulgur wheat
    - 1/2 cup parsley, chopped
    - 1/4 cup tomatoes, diced
    - 1 tbsp olive oil

Instructions:

1. Marinate chicken in olive oil, lemon juice, and oregano for 1 hour. Grill for 5 minutes per side.
2. Blend hummus ingredients until smooth.
3. Mix tabbouleh ingredients and let rest for 30 minutes.
4. Serve grilled chicken with hummus and tabbouleh.

Roasted Cornish Game Hen with Herb Butter

Ingredients:

- 1 Cornish game hen
- 2 tbsp butter, softened
- 1 tsp fresh rosemary, chopped
- 1 tsp fresh thyme, chopped
- 1 clove garlic, minced
- 1/2 tsp salt
- 1/2 tsp black pepper

Instructions:

1. Preheat oven to 400°F (200°C).
2. Mix butter with rosemary, thyme, garlic, salt, and pepper. Rub under the hen's skin.
3. Roast for 45–50 minutes, basting occasionally, until golden brown.

Gochujang Glazed Pork Belly with Sesame Rice

Ingredients:

- 1 lb pork belly, sliced
- 1 tbsp gochujang (Korean chili paste)
- 1 tbsp soy sauce
- 1 tbsp honey
- 1 tsp sesame oil
- **For Rice:**
    - 1 cup cooked rice
    - 1 tsp sesame seeds
    - 1 green onion, sliced

Instructions:

1. Mix gochujang, soy sauce, honey, and sesame oil.
2. Coat pork belly in the mixture and bake at 375°F (190°C) for 40 minutes.
3. Mix rice with sesame seeds and green onion, then serve with pork belly.

Grilled Octopus with Lemon & Olive Oil

Ingredients:

- 1 lb octopus tentacles
- 1/2 tsp salt
- 1/4 cup olive oil
- 1 tbsp lemon juice
- 1 tsp oregano

Instructions:

1. Boil octopus in salted water for 45 minutes, then drain.
2. Grill tentacles over high heat for 3 minutes per side.
3. Toss with olive oil, lemon juice, and oregano before serving.

www.ingramcontent.com/pod-product-compliance
Lightning Source LLC
LaVergne TN
LVHW081459060526
838201LV00056BA/2837